The Sky Is Full of Stars

THIS IS A LET'S-READ-AND-FIND-OUT SCIENCE BOOK

THE SKY IS FULL OF STARS

by Franklyn M. Branley   *Illustrated by Felicia Bond*

Thomas Y. Crowell New York

Other Let's-Read-and-Find-Out Science Books *You Will Enjoy*

The Beginning of the Earth by Franklyn M. Branley • *The Big Dipper* by Franklyn M. Branley • *Eclipse* by Franklyn M. Branley • *Energy from the Sun* by Melvin Berger • *Light and Darkness* by Franklyn M. Branley • *The Planets in Our Solar System* by Franklyn M. Branley • *The Moon Seems to Change* by Franklyn M. Branley • *The Sun: Our Nearest Star* by Franklyn M. Branley • *Sunshine Makes the Seasons* by Franklyn M. Branley • *What Makes Day and Night* by Franklyn M. Branley

Let's-Read-and-Find-Out Science Books are edited by Dr. Roma Gans, Professor Emeritus of Childhood Education, Teachers College, Columbia University, and by Dr. Franklyn M. Branley, Astronomer Emeritus and former Chairman of The American Museum-Hayden Planetarium. For a complete catalog of *Let's-Read-and-Find-Out Science Books,* write to Thomas Y. Crowell, Department 363, 10 East 53rd Street, New York, New York 10022.

Library of Congress Cataloging in Publication Data

Branley, Franklyn Mansfield, 1915–
  The sky is full of stars.

  (A Let's-read-and-find-out book)
  Summary: Explains how to view stars and ways to locate star pictures, known as constellations, through-out the year.
    1. Stars—Juvenile literature. [1. Stars.
  2. Constellations] I. Bond, Felicia, ill. II. Title.
  QB801.7.B73 1981   523.8   81-43037.
  ISBN 0-690-04118-7   AACR2
  ISBN 0-690-04119-5 (lib. bdg.)

1 2 3 4 5 6 7 8 9 10
First Edition

Grateful acknowledgement is made to Palomar Observatory, California Institute of Technology, for the photographs on pages 3 and 25 and to Helmut Wimmer for the star maps on pages 16, 20, 22, and 26.

The Sky Is Full of Stars

On a clear, dark night, go outside and look at
the stars. Stars are to the east of you and to the
west. Stars are north of you and south of you.
Stars are overhead. They are all around you.
The sky is full of stars.

There is one star you cannot
see at night. It is the sun. The
sun is our daytime star.

All of the stars are far, far away.

Many stars are so far away you cannot see
them without a telescope.

Some stars are so far away you cannot see
them even with the biggest telescope in the world.

3

When you first look at the sky, the stars may
all seem alike to you. But take your time, look for
a while, and you will begin to see differences.

Some stars are brighter than others. You may
see half a dozen or so that are very bright.

If it's a very clear night, you may see that stars
have colors. You may see that some stars are white,
some are red, some are blue, and some are yellow.

You may see stars that are in one part of the
sky early in the evening have moved to another
part later that same night. That is because stars
rise and set just as the sun does.

When a star is rising, it is in the eastern sky. Later
on that night, the star will be in the western sky.
It will set below the horizon, just as the sun does.

At different times of the year, you will see
different stars in the sky.

On a clear night in December, you might see a
very bright blue star. Its name is Sirius.

But if you looked for Sirius in June, you
wouldn't be able to find it. On June nights, Sirius
is on the other side of the world.

Summer stars are different from winter stars.

People who lived long ago looked at the stars a
lot. They saw groups of stars in the sky. They
imagined that the groups made pictures.

They saw a lion in the sky, a bull, a hunter, a

rabbit, a big dog and a little one, birds, fishes, and other things.

Now we call the star-pictures constellations. In the whole sky there are 88 constellations.

Have you ever tried to find the constellations?
One of them is the Great Bear. You may already
have seen a part of it, the part that is called the
Big Dipper. The Big Dipper is easy to find, but it
is harder to see the rest of the bear—its feet and
legs and head.

When you look for the constellations, you must
use your imagination, just as people did long ago.

13

Suppose you were to start in February at about
9 P.M. It's dark by then, so you can see the stars.
Go outside and face south. To find which way

is south, just remember where the sun sets. It
sets in the western sky. Stand so your right side
is toward the west. You will be facing south.

As you look south, you will see seven bright stars quite high in the sky. They are a part of the constellation called Orion. Orion is the brightest constellation in the winter sky.

Ancient stargazers thought this group of stars looked like a hunter. They called the two bright

If you stargaze in January, Orion will be a bit toward your left at 9 P.M. In March, it will be a bit toward your right.

stars at the top of the constellation the shoulders of Orion. Above the shoulders are dimmer stars that make an arm of Orion and his club. In his left hand, Orion holds a shield. The two bright stars at the bottom of the constellation are his knees. The three bright middle stars are his belt.

The stars that make Orion's belt are called
Alnitak, Alnilam, and Mintaka. Some of the
names of stars sound strange to us. That is
because they are not English words. Hundreds of
years ago the Arabs and Persians named many of

the stars. Today we still use many of those names.
February is also a good time to look for Sirius.
It will be to the left of Orion and a little below it.
Sirius is the brightest star in the night sky. It is
brighter than all the other stars, except the sun.

In springtime, you will see different stars. In the middle of April, face south at about 9 P.M. Look for a bright star. It will be almost directly in front of you and quite high up in the sky. The star is called Regulus.

A little above Regulus, look for five stars in the shape of a question mark turned backward. The

If you look for Leo in March, it will be a bit toward your left at 9 P.M. In May it will be a bit toward your right.

question mark is the head of the constellation called Leo, the lion—the main constellation of spring. Regulus is the heart of the lion.

To the left of Regulus you will see three stars that make a triangle. One of the stars is a bit brighter than the other two. It marks the tail end of the lion.

The middle of August
is a good time to see the
stars of summer. As soon
as it's dark, look south.
You will see three bright
stars high in the sky: Vega,
Deneb, and Altair. Each is
in a different constellation.
    The star to the right,
Vega, is the brightest star in

the constellation Lyra. Lyra means lyre, a small stringed instrument used long ago.

The bright star to the left of Vega, and a bit above it is Deneb. Deneb is in the constellation Cygnus, the swan. Lower down is the bright star Altair. It is in the constellation Aquila, the eagle.

If you look for Lyra, Cygnus, and Altair in July, they will be a bit toward your left at 9 P.M. In September, they will be a bit toward your right.

If the sky is dark and clear, you will be able to see the Milky Way. Summer is the best time to see it. People used to think it was a weather cloud. It looked milky and that's why they gave it the name.

Later, when people looked at the Milky Way through a telescope, they discovered that it is really billions and billions of stars. The stars are very far away and very dim. They seem to blend together into a cloud—a cloud of stars.

25

At about 9 P.M. in October, face south. Nearly
overhead you will see four bright stars. They
make a square. They are the body of a very
unusual horse. This horse is upside down, and it

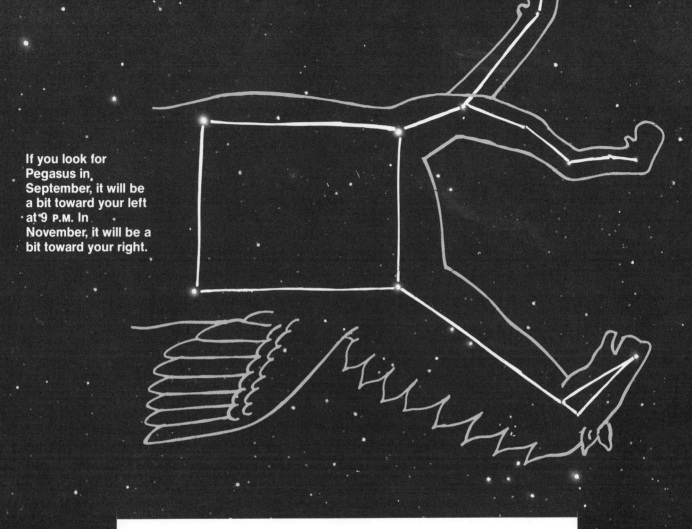

If you look for Pegasus in September, it will be a bit toward your left at 9 P.M. In November, it will be a bit toward your right.

has wings. It is the constellation Pegasus, the flying horse. Look at the picture to see where its head, legs, and wings are. That will help you find them in the sky.

As you find the constellations, or even before,
you can make your own pictures of them. Ask
someone to help you cut out both ends of a coffee
can. Then cut a hole in the plastic lid that comes
with the can. The hole should be just large
enough so the end of a flashlight fits through it.

1. Cut out four pieces of cardboard, each large enough to cover the end of the coffee can.

2. Mark the stars of a constellation on each piece of cardboard.

 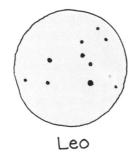 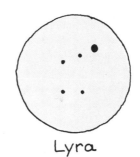 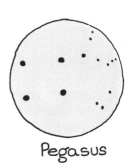

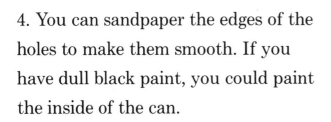

Orion   Leo   Lyra   Pegasus

3. Then use a sharp nail to punch holes through the stars. Twist the nail to make the holes as round as possible.

4. You can sandpaper the edges of the holes to make them smooth. If you have dull black paint, you could paint the inside of the can.

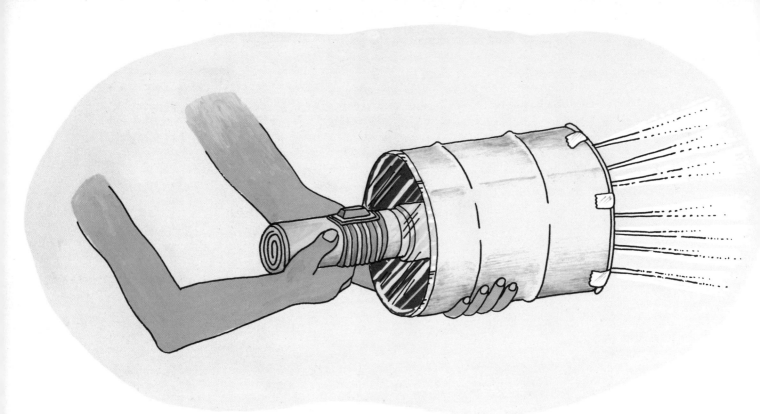

Hold or tape the cardboard over one end of the can. In a dark room, point the can at a wall or the ceiling, and turn on the flashlight.

You will see a picture of the constellation you drew. It will not be as clear and as bright as, say, Orion really is. But the picture will help you to remember the shape of the hunter in the sky.

Now you know a few of the brightest stars and
constellations in the sky. If you keep stargazing,
soon you will know your way all around the sky.
Maybe someday you'll travel all over the world,

far to the north and to the south. When you do,
you'll see more and more constellations. Someday you may see all the constellations in the
whole sky, all 88 of them. Only a few people know
them all.

About the Author

FRANKLYN M. BRANLEY, Astronomer Emeritus and former Chairman of The American Museum–Hayden Planetarium, is well known as the author of many books about astronomy and other sciences for young people of all ages. He is also coeditor of the Let's-Read-and-Find-Out Science Book series.

Dr. Branley holds degrees from New York University, Columbia University, and the State University of New York at New Paltz. He and his wife live in Sag Harbor, New York.

About the Illustrator

FELICIA BOND was born in Japan and grew up in New York and Texas. A graduate of the University of Texas, where she received a degree in Fine Arts, she has been an art teacher for children and adults, a botanical illustrator, an exhibit artist for museums, and a puppeteer. She presently lives in New York City.

Ms. Bond is the author and illustrator of a picture book, *Poinsettia and Her Family,* and the illustrator of *When Birds Change Their Feathers,* also in the Let's-Read-and-Find-Out series.